Best Friends Forever

D1176729

500

Really Funny
Jokes

M&S

Marks and Spencer plc
PO Box 3339
Chester CH99 9QS

shop online
www.marksandspencer.com

ISBN 978-1-78061-353-6
Printed in China

CONTENTS

Share these jokes for a
giggle with your friends and
family anytime!

SO COOL!

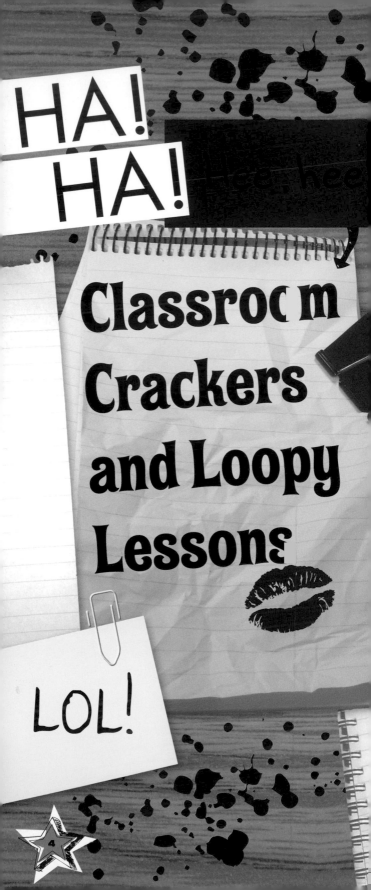

Teacher: "If I took four oranges and cut them into quarters, then added 14 grapes, what would I get?"

Ravi: "Fruit salad, miss."

Teacher: "What did you write your project on?"

Oliver: "Paper."

What should you eat on sports day?
Runner beans.

What's a butterfly's favourite subject? Mothematics!

What's the largest table in school?

THE MULTIPLICATION TABLE.

Teacher: "If I gave you three hamsters, and the next day gave you three more, how many would you have?"
Ruby: "Seven."
Teacher: "Seven?"
Ruby: "Yes, I've got one already."

Teacher: "Jack, are you sleeping in my class?"
Jack: "Not any more, Miss!"

Teacher: "If you had £5 and you asked your dad for another £5, how much would you have?"
Jack: "Five pounds."
Teacher: "You don't know how to add up!"
Jack: "You don't know my dad."

What do elves learn in school? The elf-abet.

Teacher: "Tell me an animal that lives in Lapland."
Charlie: "A reindeer."
Teacher: "Good, now tell me another one."
Charlie: "Another reindeer!"

Why is it dangerous to do sums in the jungle?
Because if you add four and four, you get ate!

What's a snake's best subject?
Hiss-tory.

What's a cow's favourite subject? Moo-sic!

How do dinosaurs pass exams? With extinc

Why was the cannibal expelled from school? He kept buttering up the teacher.

What's a bird's favourite subject? Owl-gebra!

Alex: "Dad, can you help me find the answer for my maths homework?"

Dad: "Is it still missing? I remember looking for it when I was at school!"

Teacher: "Who built the Ark?"
Jess: "I have Noah idea!"

Dad: "Why aren't you doing very well in history?"
George: "Because the teacher keeps asking about things that happened before I was born!"

What's a pirate's favourite subject?

Arrrr-t!

Teacher: "If there are eight cats in a basket and one jumps out, how many are left?"
Ed: "None. The rest were copycats!"

Teacher: "Where would you find Hadrian's Wall?"
Tom: "Around Hadrian's garden, Sir?"

Teacher: "Why was Oliver Cromwell buried in Westminster Abbey?"
Joseph: "Because he was dead."

What's the fastest country in the world? Rush-a!

TEACHER: "WHERE WAS THE MAGNA CARTA SIGNED?"
LILY: "AT THE BOTTOM!"

Teacher: "What happened at the Boston Tea Party?"
Grace: "I don't know, I wasn't invited."

**Teacher: "Did the Ancient Romans hunt bears?"
Edward: "Not in the winter, if they had any sense."**

Where do fish come from? Fin-land.

WHAT iS THE HEALTHiEST LESSON? HiSTORY, BECAUSE iT'S FULL OF DATES.

What do you call Australian boxer shorts? Down-underwear!

Teacher: "Is eating chicken good for your health?"
Dan: "Not if you're a chicken."

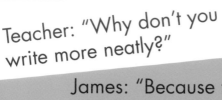

Teacher: "Why don't you write more neatly?"

James: "Because then you'll be able to see that I can't spell!"

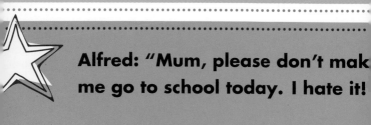

Alfred: "Mum, please don't mak me go to school today. I hate it!

Mum: "You have to go – after all, you are the headmaster!"

Where do ponies come from? Horse-tralia.

Where do sea mammals come from? WHALES.

pssst, something funny!

What do you call someone who keeps talking when no one is listening?

A teacher.

Why was the teacher cross-eyed?
She couldn't control her pupils.

Teacher: "Did you take a bath this morning?"
Luke: "No, is there one missing?"

Where do polar bears come from?

CHiLLY.

Joe (to music teacher): "What would you like me to play?"
Teacher: "Truant!"

Where do pigs come from? **Ham-erica.**

HILARIOUS!

Teacher: "Why can't you answer any of my questions?"
Emily: "Well, if I could there wouldn't be much point in me being here!"

Where do girls come from?

Skirt-land.

Where do wasps come from?
Sting-apore.

Teacher: "Where is the English Channel?"
Pupil: "I don't know, I haven't got digital TV!"

Jack: "My teacher's an angel."
Alfie: "You're lucky. Mine's still alive!"

Teacher: "If you put your hand in your left pocket and found £1.75 and then put your hand in your right pocket and found £2.50, what would you have?"
Harry: "Somebody else's trousers on!"

Where do pigeons come from?
Coo-lumbia

Teacher: "This homework is in your mum's handwriting!"
Ethan: "I know, I borrowed her pen."

Teacher: "What is a duchess?"
Joe: "I dunno – is it different to an English 's'?"

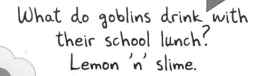
What do goblins drink with their school lunch? Lemon 'n' slime.

Teacher: "I hope I didn't see you looking at Jack's answers!"

Harry: "I hope you didn't, too."

Teacher: "You've got your shoes on the wrong feet."

Bella: "These are the only feet I've got, Miss."

Teacher: "Lewis, did you miss school yesterday?"
Lewis: "No, I didn't miss it at all!"

Teacher: "Which word is always spelt wrong?"
Lily: "Wrong!"

HEE HEE HEE HEE

Where do you go to learn how to make ice cream? Sundae school!

Teacher: "You aren't paying attention to me. Are you having trouble hearing?"
Sophie: "No, Miss – I'm having trouble listening."

Arnie: "My teacher was bitten by a dog yesterday."
Ben: "How is she?"
Arnie: "She's fine, but the dog died"

17

Guaranteed to get you
GIGGLING!

Why was Cinderella dropped from the school football team? Because she ran away from the ball.

Teacher: "Name a liquid that will never freeze."
Samuel: "Hot water."

Teacher: "You should have been here at 9 o'clock."
Tom: "Why, did something exciting happen?"

Teacher: "What do you find at the end of a rainbow?"
Callum: "The letter 'w'."

What do you call
the biggest bully
in the playground?
Lord of the Swings.

Teacher: "Dylan, stop humming
while you're working!"
Dylan: "I'm not working,
Miss, just humming!"

Why did the thermometer
go to college?
Because he wanted to
get a degree.

Teacher: "What do you call
a tree that loses its leaves?"
Hannah: "Careless?"

Teacher: "What time did you
wake up this morning, Joe?"
Joe: "About 10 minutes after
I got to school, Sir!"

19

Why is school like a shower?

One wrong turn and you're in hot water.

Teacher: "You weren't at school yesterday, Alex. I heard you were at the cinema."

Alex: "That's not true – I've got the tickets from the football match to prove it!"

Why did the kid walk backwards to school?

It was back-to-school day.

Hee hee!

Teacher: "Why are you always late for school?"
Matthew: "Because you always ring the bell before I get here!"

LOL!

Teacher: "This essay about your pet parrot is exactly the same as the one your sister handed in!"
Amelia: "Yes, Miss, it's the same parrot."

SO
FUNNY

Teacher: "What was the Romans' most remarkable achievement?"
Ellie: "Learning Latin!"

What did the dinosaur have for lunch at school?
The headteacher.

21

Dad: "What did you learn today?"

Daniel: "I learned that those sums you did for me were wrong."

Charlie: "I've been banned from cookery lessons because I burned something."
Mum: "What did you burn?"
Charlie: "I burned the school down."

What did the bookworm say to the librarian? "Can I burrow this book, please?"

Harvey: "How many teachers work at this school?"
Henry: "About half of them!"

What insect is good at maths?
An account-ant.

Teacher: "If an apple a day keeps the doctor away, what does an onion do?"
Freddy: "Keeps everyone away!"

22

Ryan: "How did you manage to get that black eye?"
Jamie: "You see that tree in the playground?"
Ryan: "Yes."
Jamie: "Well, I didn't."

Teacher: "I hear you've been telling everyone that I'm boring."
Harrison: "Sorry, I didn't know it was meant to be a secret."

Teacher: "Why are a lot of famous artists Dutch?"

Tom: "Because they were born in Holland!"

Teacher: "That story's excellently written for someone your age!"
Ella: "How about for someone my mum's age?"

Who would you find on a haunted beach during the school holidays?
Sand-witches.

HOW DID THE VIKINGS SEND SECRET MESSAGES? BY NORSE CODE.

Dad: "How were the exam questions?"
Molly: "Fine."
Dad: "Why are you crying then?"
Molly: "The questions were fine. The answers were the problem."

What do you call a Victorian ant?

An antique.

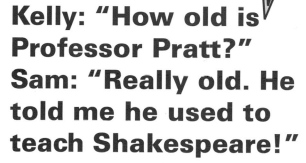

Kelly: "How old is Professor Pratt?"
Sam: "Really old. He told me he used to teach Shakespeare!"

Teacher: "Are you good at arithmetic?"
Nathan: "Well, yes and no."
Teacher: "What do you mean, yes and no?"
Nathan: "Yes, I'm no good at arithmetic."

Why did the chicken cross the playground? To get to the other slide.

Lisa (on phone): "Lisa has a bad cold and won't be able to come to school today."
School secretary: "Who is this?"
Lisa: "This is my mum speaking."

Mum: "What did you learn in school today?"
Will: "How to write."
Mum: "What did you write?"
Will: "I don't know, they haven't taught us how to read yet!"

Where do ghosts do their homework?

Exorcise books.

Abigail: "my teacher gave me a detention for something I didn't do!"
Mum: "That's terrible. What didn't you do?"
Abigail: "my homework."

Jake: "Someone threw a stink bomb into the boys' toilets today."
Mum: "How did it smell?"
Jake: "Much better!"

Why was the maths book unhappy?
Because it had loads of problems.

Holly: "Why are you going to night school?"
Heidi: "To learn how to read in the dark!"

What did the alien say to the school librarian? "Take me to your reader."

Laughing Stock and Cross Porpoises

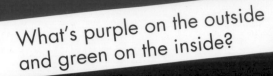

What's purple on the outside and green on the inside?

The Incredible Hulk wearing purple pyjamas.

Why did the safari guide lose his driving licence?

He parked on a yellow lion.

What do you call a bear with no ear?
A 'b'.

Why can you never swindle a snake?
Because it's impossible to pull its leg.

How do you know if there's a woolly mammoth in your bed? All the duvet is taken.

Why do woolly mammoths have trunks? Because they would look silly with glove compartments.

What does it tell you when you see three polar bears walking down the street wearing blue sweatshirts? They're all on the same team.

Did you hear about the cat that swallowed a ball of yarn? She had mittens.

Cute

Why can't skeletons play music in church? They have no organs.

What did the bald man say when he got a comb for his birthday?

"Thanks, I'll never part with it."

Why did the clock get angry?

It was wound up.

What's the difference between a mosquito and a fly?

A mosquito can fly, but a fly can't mosquito.

What do you call a parrot wearing a raincoat?
Polly unsaturated.

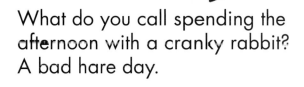

What do you call spending the afternoon with a cranky rabbit?
A bad hare day.

What do you get when you drop a piano down a mineshaft?
A-flat minor.

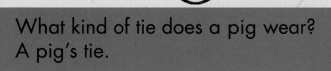

What kind of tie does a pig wear?
A pig's tie.

What's the best time to go to the dentist?
Two thirty (tooth hurty).

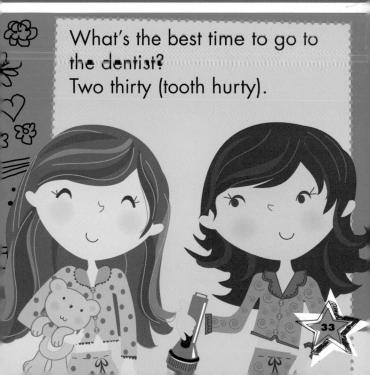

What do you get if you cross a woolly mammoth with a whale? A submarine with a built-in snorkel.

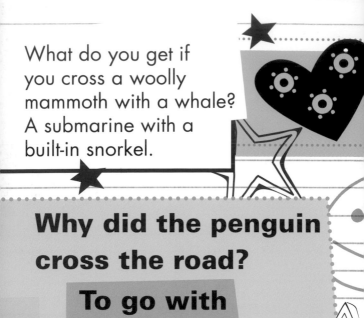

Why did the penguin cross the road?

To go with the floe.

What do penguins take to school?

Ice-pack lunch.

WAY COOL

Why don't penguins carry fish in their pockets?

Because they don't have pockets.

Why are penguins popular on the Internet?

Because they have web feet.

Did you hear about the hyena that swallowed the gravy granules?

He made a laughing stock of himself.

Why did the boy try to take his nose apart in winter?

He wanted to see what made it run.

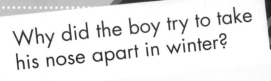

Why are penguins good racing drivers? Because they're always in pole position.

What do you call a gigantic polar bear? Nothing, you just run away.

Where do penguins keep their money? In the snow bank.

What kind of man doesn't like to sit in front of the fire? The Abominable Snowman.

HILARIOUS

Why was the pelican kicked out of the hotel? Because he had a big bill.

Where does money fall like snow? Wherever there's a change in the weather.

What do you call a yeti in a phone box? Stuck.

What do you get if you cross a yeti with a kangaroo? A fur coat with big pockets.

THAT IS SO FUNNY

Total fun!

**More jokes to share
with your best mates!**

How did the yeti feel when
he had flu?
Abominable.

What do yetis eat on
top of Everest?
High tea.

What animal talks too much?
A yak.

What do yetis call
their offspring?
Chill-dren.

What do cows do on
Saturday nights?
Go to the moooooovies.

How do robins get in shape?
They do worm-ups.

What is brown, has a hump and
lives at the North Pole?
A very lost camel.

Name six things smaller than an
ant's mouth.
Six of its teeth.

What do you call angry dolphins?
Cross porpoises.

GIRLY
GIGGLES

Where do horses go when they are sick?
To the horsepital.

What did the boy octopus say to the girl octopus?
I want to hold your hand, hand, hand, hand, hand, hand, hand, hand.

What's big, yellow and eats polar bears?
A big, yellow polar bear eater.

What kind of car does a cat drive?
A Cat-a-lac.

Totally cool!

What did the scientist say when he found bones on the moon? "The cow didn't make it."

What do sharks eat with their peanut butter? Jellyfish.

MMMMM

LOVE IT!

What's the difference between a piano and a fish? You can tune a piano, but you can't tuna fish.

KEEP YOUR FRIENDS GIGGLING

**What did one casket say to the other casket?
"Is that you coffin?"**

What do you get if you cross a duck with a rooster?
A bird that wakes you up at the quack of dawn.

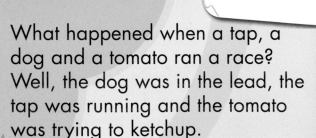

What happened when a tap, a dog and a tomato ran a race?
Well, the dog was in the lead, the tap was running and the tomato was trying to ketchup.

What did the birthday balloon say to the pin?
"Hi, Buster."

Where do monkeys make toast?
Under a gorilla (grill-a).

What do you get if you cross a chocolate bar with an elk?
A chocolate mousse.

What do you get if you sit under a cow?
A pat on the head.

Where do tough chickens come from? Hard-boiled eggs.

What do you call a camel with no humps? Humphrey.

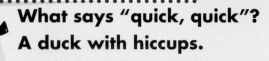

What says "quick, quick"? A duck with hiccups.

What do nuclear scientists like to eat? Fission chips.

What is yellow and very dangerous?
Shark-infested custard.

What did the zero say to the eight?
"Nice belt."

What's black and white and read all over?
A newspaper.

LOViN' THE LAUGHS!

How do mountains hear?
They have mountaineers.

What would you do if you broke your leg in two places?

Stay away from those places in future.

What do you get if you cross a polar bear with a flower?

I don't know, but I'm not going to smell it.

Why was the seal swimming backstroke?

It had just had lunch and didn't want to swim on a full stomach.

Is it better to write with your right or left hand?

Ideally, you should be writing with a pen, not a hand.

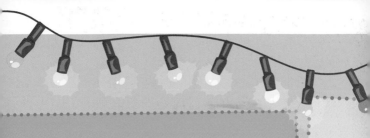

What did the traffic light say to the car?

"Don't look now, I'm changing."

Why did the snowman die with his boots on?

Because he didn't want to stub his toe when he kicked the bucket.

Do moths cry?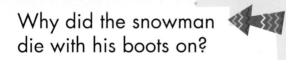

Sure. Haven't you ever seen a moth bawl?

Have you ever seen a man-eating polar bear?

No, but in a cafe I once saw a man eating chicken.

Can you spell eighty in two letters?
A. T.

What happens if you throw a red ruby in the Black Sea?
It gets wet.

What do you get if you cross a cricket ball and an alien?
A bowling green.

Why did the farmer plough his field with a steamroller?
He wanted to grow mashed potatoes.

How do you know you are being haunted by a parrot?
It keeps saying "Ooo's a pretty boy then?"

★

What did the big weevil say to the little weevil?
"You're the lesser of two weevils."

★

What do you get if you cross a chemical with a bicycle?
Bike carbonate of soda.

Why did the stupid boy wear a turtleneck jumper?
To hide his flea collar.

★

Why did the coffee taste like mud?
Because it was ground
that morning.

What do you do if you split
your sides laughing?
Run till you get a stitch.

Why do rabbits
eat rust?
Because it's a type of
car rot.

Why is a shirt with eight
buttons so interesting?
Because you fasten eight
(fascinate).

What happens when a
thousand labourers fall off
a mountain?
You get a navvy-lanche.

What do you call
a gorilla <u>with</u> bananas
in its ears?
Anything you like,
it can't hear you.

How <u>does</u> Luke Skywalker
get from planet to planet?
Ewoks (he walks).

How can you make
seven even?
Take away the letter 's'.

What do you get hanging
from trees in the jungle?
Sore arms.

What happened to the man who
couldn't tell the difference between
soap and putty?
His armpits stuck together
and all his windows fell out.

How do you make a lemon drop?
Let go of it.

What does a dentist
call his X-rays?
Tooth pics.

LOL

Muscle Sprouts and Scream Cheese

What's the best way to see flying saucers?
Trip up the waitress.

What do monsters have on their toast?
Scream cheese.

Why did the baby strawberry cry? Because his parents were in a jam.

What is a nun's favourite food?
Angel cake.

Why did the cheese play roulette all night?
Because he was on a roll.

"Waitress, do you serve crabs?"
"Certainly, Sir – we serve anyone."

What are the strongest vegetables in the world? Muscle sprouts.

"Waiter, this soup tastes funny."
"So why aren't you laughing?"

What is James Bond's favourite food? Mince spies.

"Waiter, will my pizza be long?"
"No, it'll be round, the same as everyone else's!"

How do you make
fairy cakes?
With elf-raising flour.

Customer: "What's this?"
Waiter: "It's a banana surprise."
Customer: "I can't see
any bananas."
Waiter: "I know, Sir, that's
the surprise."

**Mum: "Eat your spinach, it'll
put colour in your cheeks."
Max: "But I don't want
green cheeks!"**

Knock, knock.

Who's there?

Orange.

Orange who?

**Orange you going to
let me in?**

"Waiter, do you have frogs' legs?"
"No, Sir, I've always walked like this."

What's a Frenchman's favourite pudding? Trifle tower.

Why did the bacon groan? Because the egg's yolks were so bad.

How does a penguin make pancakes? With its flippers.

57

Waiter: "How did you find your dinner?"
Customer: "With a magnifying glass."

What sits in the corner of the room and wobbles?
A jelly-vision.

What happened to the man who stole an apple pie?
He was taken into custard-y.

A man who works in a butcher's shop is 6 feet tall and wears size 11 shoes. What does he weigh?
Meat.

Why did the lettuce blush?
He saw the salad dressing.

Why did the grape go out with a prune?
Because he couldn't get a date.

"Waiter, there's a flea in my soup."
"Well, tell it to hop it."

What's the difference between British ice cream and American ice cream?
About 5,000 kilometres.

"Waiter, there's a fly in my soup!"
"Don't worry, Sir, the spider in your salad will eat it."

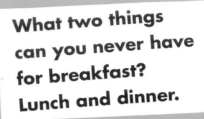

What two things can you never have for breakfast? Lunch and dinner.

"Waiter, there's a fly in my coffee."
"That's all right, Sir, he won't drink much."

Why did the bagel go to the dentist?
Because it needed a filling.

"Waiter, there's a small slug in this lettuce."
"Sorry, Sir, I'll just go and get you a bigger one."

"Waiter, there's a fly swimming in my soup." "What do you expect me to do? Call a lifeguard?"

What's a porcupine's favourite food?
Prickled onions.

What is a taxi driver's favourite food?
Corn on the cab.

Knock, knock.
Who's there?
Noah.
Noah who?
Noah way to the nearest burger bar?

How do you make a sausage roll?
Push it off your plate.

"Waiter, how are your mussels today?"
"A bit sore, Sir – I was playing football last night."

LOVIN' THE LAUGHS!

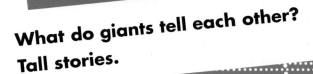

**What do giants tell each other?
Tall stories.**

"Waiter, is there spaghetti
on the menu?"
"Yes, I'll just get a cloth and
wipe it off."

Eww

**What does a
dustbin man have
for lunch?
Junk food.**

Tom: "What've you got in
your truck?"
Farmer: "Horse manure."
Tom: "What are you going
to do with it?"
Farmer: "Put it on
my strawberries."
Tom: "Try cream and sugar
– it tastes much better."

63

What do you call a train full of caramels?
A chew-chew train.

What's the best place to find diamonds?
In a pack of cards.

What did the nut say when it sneezed?
"Ca-shew!"

Did you hear about the fight in the chip shop last night?
Two fish got battered.

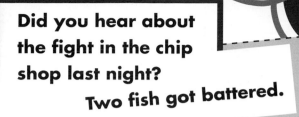

YUCK

"Waiter, there's a dead fly in my soup."
"Looks like he's committed insecticide!"

"Waiter, how long will my sausages be?"
"About ten to twelve centimetres if you're lucky!"

What happens if you eat yeast and shoe polish?
You'll rise and shine every morning.

"Waiter, how often do you change the tablecloths in this restaurant?"
"I don't know, Sir, I've only been here six months."

Mum: "Why are you shivering?"
Sam: "Because you're making me chill[l]

How do you know carrots are good for your eyes?

Because you never see a rabbit wearing glasses.

If you hold 9 oranges in one hand and 10 lemons and 10 berries in another, what do you have?
Really big hands.

What vegetable should you never have on a boat?
A leek.

What do you get when two peas fight?
Black-eyed peas.

"Waiter, what's this insect in my soup?"
"I dunno, I'm a waiter, not an entomologist!"

"Waiter, there's a dead fly swimming in my soup."
"Don't be ridiculous, dead flies can't swim!"

Knock, knock.

Who's there?

Ice cream.

Ice cream who?

Ice cream if you don't let me in!

Test these jokes out on your friends.

TOTALLY HILARIOUS

What do golfers eat for lunch?
Club sandwiches.

Mum: "Why are you eating so fast?"
Ali: "I don't want to lose my appetite."

"Waiter, there's a button in my soup."
"Thank you, Sir. I've been looking for that everywhere."

"Waiter, there's a spider drowning in my soup."
"I don't think it's deep enough for him to drown, Sir."

Why are cooks cruel?
Because they beat eggs, whip cream and batter fish.

Why don't polar bears eat penguins?
Because they can't get the wrappers off.

"Waiter, bring me some lamb chops and make them lean."
"To the left or right, Sir?"

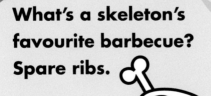

Think **FUNNY**

What's a skeleton's favourite barbecue?
Spare ribs.

What's green and wears an apron?

A cooking apple.

"Waiter, do you have frogs' legs?"
"Yes, Sir."
"Well, hop over here and take my order."

HOW DO YOU MAKE A BANANA SHAKE? TAKE IT TO A SCARY MOVIE.

Two crisps were walking down
the road when a car stopped.
"Do you want a lift?" asked the driver.
"No thanks," said one crisp,
"we're Walkers."

What is small, wobbly
and sits in a pram?

A jelly baby.

Why did the
man throw his
toast out of
the window?
To watch his
butterfly.

What's yellow
and sniffs?

A banana with a cold.

What makes
the Tower
of Pisa lean?
It doesn't
eat much.

Knock, knock.
Who's there?
Annie.
Annie who?
Annie more biscuits
left? I'm starving!

Who's there?
Pete.
Pete who?
Pizza delivery man!

KNOCK, KNOCK.

When should you feed giraffe milk to a baby?
When it's a baby giraffe.

How did the elf get indigestion?

He kept gobblin' his dinner.

Why did the potato on a motorbike get arrested?
He broke the spud limit.

What's a bear's favourite pasta?
Taglia-teddy.

72

**Why didn't the hot dog
win an Oscar?
Because he didn't get any good rolls.**

Customer: "Waiter, this restaurant must have a very clean kitchen."
Waiter: "Why?"
Customer: "Because everything tastes like soap."

"Waiter, send the chef here. I wish to complain about this disgusting meal."
"I'm afraid you'll have to wait, Sir. He's just popped out for his dinner."

Why did the polar bear eat a clock?
He was just killing time.

What's a penguin's favourite salad?
Iceberg lettuce.

Why did the T-rex eat only raw meat?

What do you get
if you cross
a prawn and
a monkey?
A shrimp-anzee.

LOL

What do you
get if you cross
a cow with
a cobra?
A milk snake.

What do you call a crate of ducks?
A box of quackers.

Farmer: "I've got a hen that lays square eggs and talks."
Ben: "That's amazing! What does she say?"
Farmer: "Ouch."

Because it didn't know how to cook!

What do you get if you cross a rabbit with a cake?
A cream bunny.

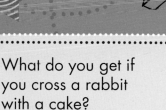

Why did the woolly mammoth eat a stupid man?
Because someone said he was nuts.

What's the fastest cake in the world? Scone!

Which great Arab invented crisps?

TEE HEE

What's the fastest vegetable?

The runner bean.

What fish is good for pudding?

A jellyfish.

What's a dog's favourite food?

Anything that's on your plate.

SULTAN VINEGAR.

What's a fish's favourite game? Name that tuna.

WOOLLY

MAMMOTHS

and Dancing YETIS

Why can't woolly mammoths ride bicycles?
Because they don't have thumbs to ring the bell.

How do fish go into business? They start on a small scale.

What do you get when you cross an ant with a yeti?
A dead ant.

To whom do fish go to borrow money?
The loan shark.

How do you describe the average cannibal?
A guy with a wife and ate children.

Which reindeer have the shortest legs?
The smallest ones.

What's the coldest creature in the sea?
A blue whale.

What do you call a fly with no wings?
A walk.

How many woolly mammoths does it take to screw in a light bulb?
Two, but you need a really big light bulb.

If athletes get athlete's foot what do astronauts get?
Mistle toe.

What did the cannibal do when he saw an all-you-can-eat restaurant?
He ate all the customers.

What did the grapes say when the monks stepped on them?
Nothing – they just let out a little whine.

What did the teacher witch do to her terrible pupil?
Ex-spelled her.

Did you hear about the cannibal who came home late for dinner?
His wife gave him an evil eye.

What did the boy do when he was offered rock cakes for tea?
He took his pick.

How do penguins drink?
Out of beak-ers.

"My dog is a nuisance. He chases everyone on a bicycle. What can I do?"
"Take his bike away."

Where do fish wash?
In a river basin.

Who has large antlers and wears white gloves? Mickey Moose.

WHAT'S WORSE THAN RAINING CATS AND DOGS? HAILING TAXIS.

What happens after a dry spell? It rains.

Why did the rhino see the film?
He really enjoyed the book.

Who's the penguin's favourite aunt?
Aunt-arctica.

What do you get if you cross a crocodile with a camera?
A snapshot.

Why shouldn't you dance with a yeti? Because you might get flat feet.

What happens to a reindeer
when it stands out in the rain?
It gets wet.

WHAT KIND
OF TREE
IS HAIRY?
A FUR
TREE.

ould you kill the Abominable
nowman just by throwing
ggs at him?
f course – he'd be eggs-terminated.

FAB JOKES

What do you get if you cross an elephant with the Abominable Snowman? A jumbo yeti.

What did the snowball do when it stopped rolling? Looked round.

Why was the Abominable Snowman's dog called Frost? Because Frost bites.

How do you stop a dog barking in the back seat of a car? Put him in the front seat.

What did one yeti say to the other? "I'm afraid I just don't believe in people."

What is the Abominable Snowman's favourite book?
'War and Frozen Peas'.

What side of a turkey do the feathers grow on?
The outside.

What did the Abominable Snowman do after he had his teeth pulled out?
He ate the dentist – whole!

When is the Arctic Ocean like a piece of string?
When a ship makes knots in it.

What do you use to cut through giant waves?
A sea-saw.

What kind of dog tells the time?
A watchdog.

What's the difference between a dog and a painter?
One sheds his coat and the other coats his shed.

Why couldn't prehistoric man send birthday cards?
The stamps kept falling off the rocks.

How do you stop a rhino from charging?

Take away its credit card.

What do you call a cow that has just had a baby? Decalfinated.

Where are there no fat people? In Finland.

Why can't a leopard hide? Because he's always spotted.

Did you hear that thieves have broken into a dogs' home? Police are following a number of leads.

SO COOL

When is a painting like a tin of sardines?

When it's done in oils.

What sort of drink would you get from a polar bear?
Iced tea.

How do rabbits send letters?
By haremail.

AB JOKES TO TELL YOUR FRIENDS★

What did one firefly say to the other when his light went out? "Give me a push, my battery is dead."

"Doctor, Doctor! I think I've swallowed a ten pound note."
"Come back tomorrow and we'll see if there's any change."

How do you know which end of a worm is its head? Tickle it and see which end laughs.

What did one candle say to the other candle? "Shall we go out tonight?"

What do you get if you cross a cat with a parrot? A carrot.

Why did the hedgehog cross the road? To see his flatmate.

What is red and stupid? A blood clot.

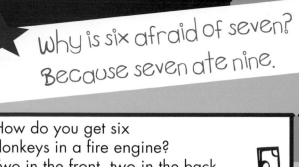

Why is six afraid of seven?
Because seven ate nine.

How do you get six
donkeys in a fire engine?
Two in the front, two in the back
and two on the top shouting,
"Eeyore, eeyore, eeyore."

**What do
footballers
drink?
Penaltea.**

What lies at the bottom of the Arctic Sea and shivers?
A NERVOUS WRECK.

How does a broom act?
With sweeping gestures.

What is white and goes up?
A confused snowflake.

What story do little ghosts like to hear at bedtime?
'Ghouldilocks and the Three Scares'.

How do you stop a cold getting to your chest?
Tie a knot in your neck.

What do you call a cat at the beach? Sandy Claws

wwww

What do you call a spaceship with its exhaust pipe hanging off?
A space racket.

Why didn't the husky dog speak to his foot? Because it's not polite to talk back to your paw.

WHAT DOES A UNiCORN CALL iTS FATHER? POPCORN.

How do you tell the difference between tinned tuna and tinned custard? Look at the labels.

What grows between your nose and your chin? Two lips (tulips).

What do comets say to each other when they meet? "Glad to meteor!"

Why was the musician arrested? He was always getting into treble.

What's sweet and cold and hurtles up the road on a stick? An articulated lolly.

What goes in pink and comes out blue? A swimmer on a cold day.

What has a black hat, flies on a broomstick and can't see? A witch with her eyes closed.

What do you call a chicken crossing the road? Poultry in motion.

WHY DID JULIUS CAESAR BUY CRAYONS? HE WANTED TO MARK ANTONY.

What shoes do you make from banana skins? Slippers.

What goes "Ooooo"? A cow with no lips.

What is everyone's favourite tree? A poplar tree.

Why is a mouse like hay? Because the cat'll (cattle) eat it.

What did the jug say to the cup? "I'll have none of your lip."

Tell these jokes to you BFF...

Haha!

98

What kind of driver doesn't need a licence? A screwdriver.

Why does a lion kneel before it springs? Because it is preying.

Did you hear about the man who crossed the Alps twice without taking a bath?

The dirty double-crosser!

What do you get if you cross a cow with a grass cutter? A lawn mooer.

...for girly giggles!

Haha!

Where did the pilgrims land when they went to America?
On their feet.

What is a sleeping bag?
A knapsack.

What did the football fan get when he listened to the match?
A burnt ear.

Why do bakers work late?
They knead the dough.

**What do you get when you cross Bambi with a ghost?
Bamboo.**

Why is Saturday night important to Julius's girlfriend?
Because that's when Julius Caesar.

What spacious car lives in a French cathedral?
The Hatchback of Notre Dame.

What makes a good librarian?
Shelf control.

Make your best friends laugh at your next sleepover!

Who drives all his customers away
but still makes a living?

A TAXI DRIVER

What tool do you use in maths lessons?
Multi-pliers.

**What's the difference
between a train and a tree?
One leaves its shed and the
other sheds its leaves.**

 What do you call a greasy chicken?
A slick chick.

Why was the little chimney ill?
It caught flu.

Why do tape machines
always win football matches?
They have fast forwards.

WHAT DO YOU CALL A CHEESE THAT ISN'T YOURS? NACHO CHEESE.

102

WHAT DO YOU GET IF YOU CROSS A SPORTS REPORTER WITH A VEGETABLE? A COMMON 'TATER.

What do ants use for hula hoops?
Cheerios.

What Roman numeral can climb a wall?
IV (ivy).

Why is Sunday stronger than Monday?
Because Monday is a weak day.

Test these jokes out on your BFFs at the next party you have!

What do you call an amusing horse racer?
A jokey.

Frying Saucers and Ridiculous Randoms

Loads more giggles for you and your friends!

Why are Martians good at gardening? Because they have green fingers.

What happened to the astronaut who reached the moon in nine minutes?

He got into the Guinness Book of Out-of-This-World Records.

Why did Chewbacca go to the doctor?
He had Star Warts.

What do you get if you cross a UFO with a rasher of bacon? A frying saucer.

105

What happened to the first restaurant on the moon?
The food was good, but the place lacked atmosphere.

What's an astronaut's favourite game?
Moon-opoly.

What did the alien say to the gardener?
"Take me to your weeder."

Where do astronauts kee their sandwiches?
In a launch box.

KEEP YOUR BFFs LAUGHING
<u>WITH THESE COOL JOKES!</u>

**What are aliens'
favourite sweets?
Martian-mallows!**

Why are astronauts
always successful?
Because they go up in the world.

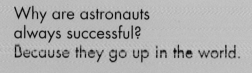

**What do you call a flea
that lives on the moon?
A lunar-tick.**

What did the Martian chef find in
his cupboard?
An unidentified frying object.

CHECK OUT THESE JOKES!

What's an alien's favourite cartoon? Lunar-tunes!

How does a Martian keep his trousers up? With an asteroid belt.

HOW FUNNY!?

LOL!

Why did the astronaut get a new job? Because he got fired.

What did the alien say
to the chef?
"Take me to your larder."

What do you call a crazy
space traveller?
An astro-nut!

What do astronauts wear
to keep warm?
Apollo neck jumpers.

WHAT DOES DOCTOR WHO
EAT WITH HIS PASTA?
DALEK BREAD.

What kind of car does
Luke Skywalker drive?
A Toy-yoda.

Where does Doctor
Who buy his cheese?
At a dalek-atessen.

How do you stop an astronaut's baby from crying?
Rocket.

Where do Martians go for a night out?
To the Mars Bar.

What was the first coffee bar in outer space?
Star-bucks!

What kind of star wears sunglasses?
A movie star!

What do you say to stop a witch laughing?
"Cut the cackle."

What did the wall say
to the other wall?
"See you at the corner."

What do you say
to a dead robot?
"Rust in peace."

Why do cats hate
flying saucers?
Because they can't
reach the milk.

What's a scientist's
favourite film?
Fission Impossible.

Where did the astronaut
leave the spaceship?
At a parking meteor.

What did dinosaurs have that no other animals ever had?
Baby dinosaurs.

Why didn't the dinosaur cross the road?
There weren't any roads in those days.

What did dinosaurs use to cut down trees?
Dinosaws.

What do you call a terrified dinosaur?
Nervous Rex.

Toby: "How would you feel if you saw a dinosaur in your garden?"
Tyler: "Very old!"

What do you get if you cross a Martian with a golf score?
A little green bogey.

Why did Granny put wheels on her rocking chair?
She liked to rock and roll.

Where do you find giant snails?
On the end of a giant's fingers.

Who was the first underwater spy?
James Pond.

WHAT DO YOU GET WHEN YOU CROSS A FISH WITH AN ELEPHANT? SWIMMING TRUNKS.

What do you get when you cross a parrot with a centipede? A walkie-talkie.

What do you get if you cross an elephant with a kangaroo? Big holes all over Australia.

What do you get if you cross a cat with a surgeon? A doctor-puss.

What do you call a dinosaur that never gives up?
A try, try, try-ceratops.

What lies on its back with one hundred feet in the air? A dead centipede.

What do you call a dinosaur with blisters?
my-feet-are-sore-us.

What would you call a dinosaur if you saw one today?
Dead!

What do you get if you cross a dinosaur with Eminem?
A rap-tor!

What do you call a dinosaur that complains all the time?
A whine-osaur.

WHAT DO YOU GET IF YOU CROSS A SKUNK WITH A BEAR?
WINNIE THE POOH.

How do you start a flea race?
One, two, flea, go!

WHAT DO YOU GET IF YOU
CROSS A DOG AND A FROG
A CROAKER SPANIEL.

What do you do when two snails
have a fight?
Leave them to slug it out.

What has antlers and
sucks blood?
A moose-quito!

Why was the baby ant
so confused?
Because all its uncles were a

What do you call a bee that is always complaining
A grumble bee.

Why did the bees go on strike?
For more honey and shorter flowers.

Why couldn't the butterfly go to the party?
It was a moth ball.

What did the woodworm
say to the chair?
"It's been nice gnawing you."

WHERE DID THE STUPID
WOODWORM LIVE?
IN A BRICK.

What do you get if you cross a
duck with a box of matches?
A fire-quacker.

How do snails get their
shells so shiny?
They use snail varnish.

Which insect makes films?
Steven Spielbug.

What is a bee with
a low buzz?
A mumble bee.

What do you call a flying skunk?

A smelly-copter.

LOL!

Where do tadpoles go to change?
The croakroom.

Haha!

LOOKIN' GOOD!

What is red and dangerous?

Strawberry and tarantula jelly.

WHAT'S BIG AND GREY AND HAS TROUBLE WITH PERSONAL HYGIENE?

A SMELLEPHANT.

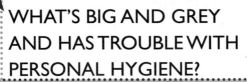

GIRLY GIGGLES!

Why are giraffes so cheap to feed?
A little goes a long way.

How do you get a hippo to the top of an oak tree?

Strap it to an acorn and wait fifty years.

Why do elephants have trunks?
They'd never fit all their clothes in a suitcase.

What do you call a man who was born in France, lived in Spain and died in England? Dead.

Charlotte: "I just flew in from New York."

What's a snowman's favourite song? Freeze a Jolly Good Fellow.

Why don't polar bears buy shoes? Because when they wear them they still have bear feet.

What do you get if you cross a river and a stream? Wet!

Tourist: "How do I get to Wembley Stadium?"
Police officer: "Keep up the training, Sir."

: "Really? Your arms
ust be killing you!"

SHARING JOKES WITH FRIENDS IS SO FUN!

What do you call a snowman in the Sahara desert? A puddle.

Why did the beach blush?
Because the sea weed.

MATT: "HAVE YOU EVER HUNTED BEAR?"
GRANDAD: "NO, BUT I'VE BEEN FISHING IN SHORTS!"

Mum: "Why did you put a mouse in Auntie's bed?"
George: "Because I couldn't find a spider."

Mum: "Why are you carrying that umbrella?"
Ellie: "Because it can't walk."

Uncle Dave: "You're very quiet, Joe."
Joe: "Well, Mum paid me to not say anything about your massive nose."

Mum: "Harry, you've been in a fight – you've lost your front teeth!"
Harry: "No I haven't, Mum. They're in my pocket."

Lucas: "Gran, why do you keep going to look at the letterbox?"
Gran: "Because my computer keeps telling me I've got mail."

Lily: "Mum, why do I have to go to bed?"
Mum: "Because the bed won't come to you."

When do mice follow cats?
In a dictionary.

Why did the chicken cross
the web?
To get to the other site.

Alex: "I wouldn't
want to be in your shoes."
Dad: "Why not?"
Alex: "They're too big for me."

Nathan: "Gran, why have you got
custard in one ear and jelly in
the other?"
Gran: "Speak up, dear.
I'm a trifle deaf."

Dad: "What's on the TV?"
Sam: "A bowl of fruit and a vase."

Dad: "Where's your school report?"
Ben: "I haven't got it."
Dad: "Why not?"
Ben: "My mate borrowed it. He wanted to scare his parents."

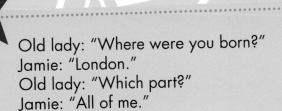

Old lady: "Where were you born?"
Jamie: "London."
Old lady: "Which part?"
Jamie: "All of me."

What starts with 'e', ends with 'e'
and only has one letter?
An envelope.

What crisps can fly?
Plain crisps.

When do computers
go to sleep?
When it's internight.

Why did the tap dancer
leave his job?
He kept falling in the sink.

What's green, very tall
and mopes in the corner?
The incredible sulk.

Why did the elephant leave the circus? He was fed up with working for peanuts.

What's an elf's favourite kind of birthday cake? Shortcake.

How do you take a lion's temperature? Very carefully.

Where do snowmen put their websites?
On the winternet.

What do you get if you cross a computer with a ballet?
The netcracker.

What do you get if you cross a telephone with a dog?
A golden receiver.

HOW CAN YOU DOUBLE YOUR MONEY?
LOOK AT IT IN A MIRROR.

128